Fish

CHRISTINE TAYLOR-BUTLER

Children's Press®
An Imprint of Scholastic Inc.
New York   Toronto   London   Auckland   Sydney
Mexico City   New Delhi   Hong Kong
Danbury, Connecticut

Content Consultant
Stephen S. Ditchkoff, PhD
Professor of Wildlife Sciences
Auburn University
Auburn, Alabama

Library of Congress Cataloging-in-Publication Data
Taylor-Butler, Christine.
 Fish / by Christine Taylor-Butler.
 pages cm.—(A true book)
 Includes bibliographical references and index.
 Audience: Ages 9–12.
 Audience: Grades 4–6.
 ISBN 978-0-531-21752-8 (lib. bdg.) — ISBN 978-0-531-22337-6 (pbk.)
 1. Fishes—Juvenile literature. I. Title.
 QL617.2.T39 2013
 597—dc23   2013001017

**Front cover: Sailfish and
a school of sardines
Back cover: Lionfish**

Find the Truth!

Everything you are about to read is true *except* for one of the sentences on this page.

Which one is **TRUE**?

T or F   Male sea horses give birth instead of females.

T or F   Whales are the largest fish on the planet.

Find the answers in this book.

3

Contents

THE BIG TRUTH!

Harvested to Extinction

A school of piranhas swims down a river in South America.

The Dubai Aquarium and Underwater Zoo houses more than 33,000 animals.

Life Underwater

Somewhere along the southern coast of Australia grows a mass of kelp and seaweed. You swim closer to get a better look. One of the leaves has eyes! This "leaf" moves among the plants as it sucks small shrimp and plankton into its snout. Dressed in leafy **camouflage**, this creature is a sea dragon. But it is not the imaginary dragon you've read about in fairy tales. This underwater dragon is a sea horse.

 The scientific name for sea horse is *Hippocampus*. It means "sea monster horse."

Dangerous Charge

Hiding in the muddy Amazon riverbed, an eel stuns a small fish with an electric pulse. Then the eel snatches the prey with its strong jaws.

The electric eel looks like a snake, but don't touch it! It can send out an electric charge equal to 600 volts. That's five times the volts in your home's electrical socket! The eel can turn the charge on or off whenever it wants.

An electric eel's charge can knock down a horse.

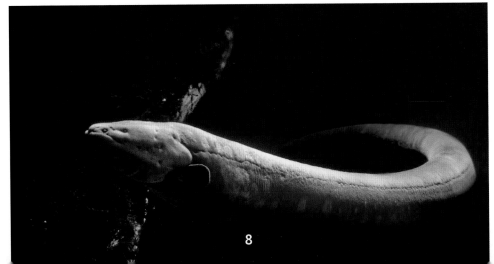

A group of cleaner wrasse goes to work cleaning a manta ray near Indonesia.

Pit Stop

Gliding above the Hawaiian coral reefs, a ray slows as it nears an underwater "cleaning station." There, a school of wrasse fish feed on the dead cells and parasites on the ray's body and gills. When the job is done, the ray swims off to hunt for food or to bury itself in sand along the ocean floor.

All of these animals have something in common. Can you guess what that is?

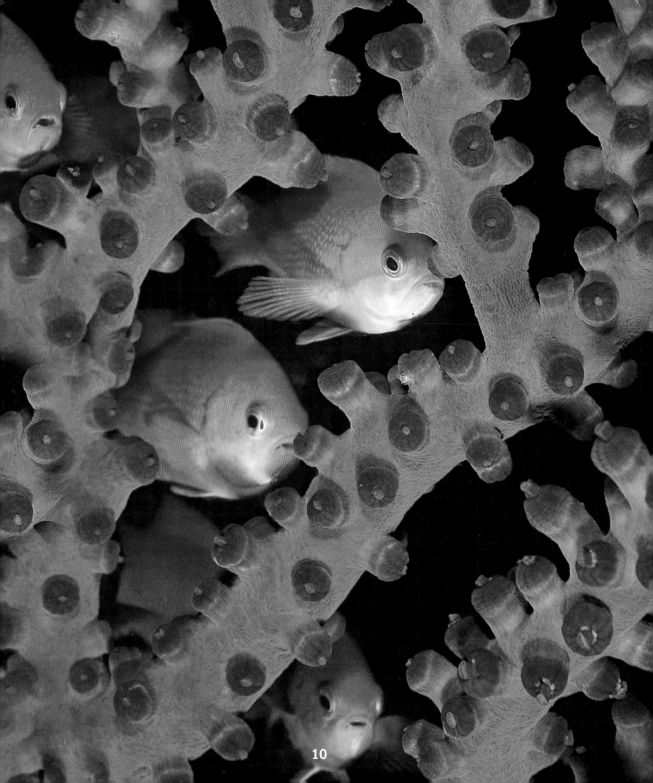

It's Classified

These animals are all fish. But what exactly is a fish? Fish are cold-blooded **vertebrates** that live underwater. As vertebrates, they have a backbone. But their bodies can't generate heat. Their body temperature is the same as the water around them. Other animals live in the water, too. But fish are the only vertebrates that have a two-chambered heart. Amphibians' and reptiles' hearts have three chambers. Mammals, such as whales and humans, have four-chambered hearts.

 There are almost 30,000 known species of fish.

Fish Family Tree

Ichthyologists are scientists who study fish. This term comes from the Greek words *ikhthus* (fish) and *logos* (to study).

Scientists use a system of classification to sort all living things. It is similar to a family tree. Fish are part of the animal kingdom. They are found in the vertebrate branch of the chart. There are two primary groups, or classes, of fish: Osteichthyes and Chondrichthyes. A third group, Agnatha, includes ancient fish without jaws.

This diver is holding a small hammerhead shark.

Quick Facts on Some Common Fish

Group (number of species)	Diet	Reproduction	Distribution	Life Span
Bony fish (28,000)	Omnivorous, eating both plants and animals	Some species are egg layers; others are live-bearers	All over the world: 58 percent in marine (salt water), 42 percent in freshwater environments	about two months–100 years, depending on the species
Sharks (400)	Carnivorous, eating only animals	Most sharks are live-bearers; 30 percent are egg layers	Saltwater oceans and seas	16–46 years
Rays (470)	Carnivorous— mostly crustaceans, worms, squid, mollusks (clams, oysters, mussels)	Most rays are live-bearers; some are egg layers	Coastal waters, tropical and temperate climates; a few species live in cold water	15–25 years
Eels (800)	Carnivorous	Egg layers	North Atlantic Ocean, coastal rivers	15 years

The ocean sunfish is the heaviest bony fish on the planet.

Bony Fish

Most fish are bony fish, which make up the Osteichthyes class. Scientists estimate that there are more than 28,000 bony fish species. Bone and **cartilage** form a bony fish's skull, jaw, backbone, and ribs. The fish breathes by passing water through its gills. Oxygen is then absorbed from the water. Bony fish are covered with overlapping scales, which are protected by a thin skin. This skin secretes a slimy mucus that shields the scales from bacteria.

Fish use their fins to swim. Pectoral fins behind the head are used for turning. Behind those, pelvic fins help the fish steer and brake while it swims. Farther back, anal fins help the fish remain stable. Dorsal fins along the back help with quick turns, and caudal fins help propel the fish forward. An air bladder inside the fish's body can be filled with air to help it stay at the same depth without effort.

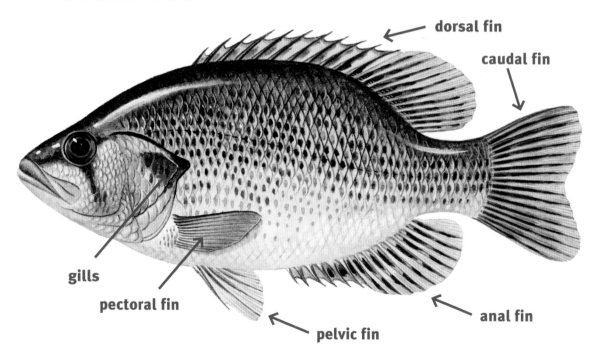

dorsal fin

caudal fin

gills

pectoral fin

anal fin

pelvic fin

Sharks and Rays

The class Chondrichthyes includes sharks and rays. Except for their bony jaws, the skeletons of these fish are made of flexible cartilage. Cartilage is softer than bone and offers little protection to their bodies. Sharks swim constantly and use their muscle contractions to circulate their blood. They don't have air bladders to keep them from sinking. Instead, their body produces oil in the liver. Oil is lighter than water, and this helps keep sharks afloat.

A shark's jaw is made of bone. This makes the jaw sturdy and strong, which is helpful when biting down on prey.

Many rays move forward by rippling their flexible fins.

Sharks and rays have nostrils, though not for breathing. Instead, the nostrils help them smell and locate prey. To breathe, sharks and rays open and close their mouths to pump water into their gills.

Rays have flexible fins, but sharks' fins are rigid. As the caudal fin pushes the shark forward, it also moves the shark downward. The shark's pectoral fins act much like a plane's wings. They give the shark lift, keeping its body level.

A moray eel, like this one, is a true eel.

Eels

There are 800 species of eels. They belong to the order Anguilliformes and are a type of bony fish. Unlike other fish, eels don't have pectoral or pelvic fins. Their dorsal fin is connected to their caudal and anal fins. Instead of scales, eels are protected by a slime coat. Like sharks and rays, eels detect their prey through their strong sense of smell. They have two sets of jaws to help them eat.

Not Really Fish

Whales are not fish. They're mammals. Fish live their entire lives in the water. Whales need to come above water to get oxygen. They would drown, just like humans, if they stayed underwater for too long.

Both whales and fish have bony skeletons. But whales are warm-blooded and can control their body temperature in cold waters. They also have four-chambered hearts. Fish are cold-blooded and have two-chambered hearts.

Habitats for Survival

Fish habitats are found in every part of the world, from the warm Amazon River to the icy waters near the polar caps. Fish live in shallow streams, swift rivers, and deep oceans. These habitats provide food and shelter, and are important to the balance of Earth's ecosystems. But a fish species cannot live in all places. A fish would die if it were moved to a drastically different environment.

Viperfish often migrate to shallow waters at night to feed.

Home Sweet Home

Piranhas can only survive in freshwater. Most sharks can only survive in salt water. Eels and rays have been found in both places.

Many fish have special adaptations for their environment. For example, in the deepest part of the ocean, soft skin and bones help fish survive the intense pressure. Other deep ocean fish glow to help them locate other fish in the dark.

Piranhas are found in the rivers of the Amazon basin.

Antarctic icefish have transparent blood because they lack red blood cells.

Antarctic icefish contain a protein that allows them to survive in freezing temperatures. It acts as an antifreeze and prevents ice crystals from forming in their blood. Some of these fish reduce their heart rate and hibernate on the ocean floor. Freshwater fish, such as koi and goldfish, also hibernate at the bottom of a pond in the winter.

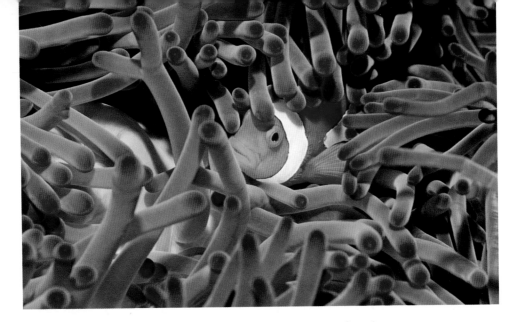

Sea anemone look like plants, but they are animals.

Some fish form partnerships with other animals. This is called **symbiosis**. Clown fish live in sea anemones. Anemone tentacles are poisonous, but not to clown fish. As a result, the anemone protects the clown fish from predators. Clown fish, in turn, eat animals that might damage the anemone.

When toxic seaweed invades coral reefs, the reefs produce a chemical that attracts gobies. The gobies rush to the area and remove the seaweed to keep their home healthy.

Hiding in Plain Sight

Some fish avoid predators by using camouflage. Ghost pipefish are often mistaken for floating sea grass. Reef stonefish look like rock and coral. The false eyespot on a butterfly fish fools predators by making the fish appear larger than it is. The cells of trumpet fish contain special pigments that allow the fish to change colors. This helps trumpet fish both get close to prey and attract a mate.

Stonefish have poisonous spines in their dorsal fins.

What's for Dinner?

Most fish are carnivores and eat animals. Some are herbivores and eat plants. A few, like koi, are omnivores. They eat both.

Most sharks are at the top of the ocean food chain. They dislocate their jaws to grab hold and take a bite out of fish, mammals, and other animals. Whale sharks may be the world's largest fish, but they eat small prey. They filter plankton and fish eggs from the ocean.

Whale sharks open their mouths wide to take in water. They filter out food and blow the water out through their gills.

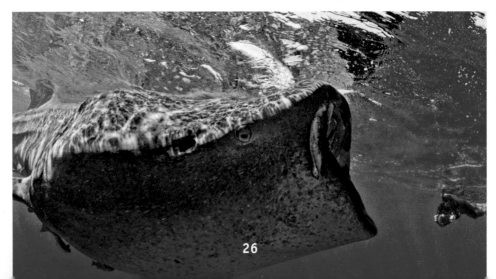

Anglerfish have been found 11,000 feet (3,353 m) below sea level.

An anglerfish's "fishing lure" juts out from the top of its head.

Rays are bottom-feeders. Their mouth is on the bottom to help them catch clams, oysters, shrimp, and fish along the ocean floor. A bony plate in the mouth grinds the food down.

Anglerfish live in total darkness. The female has a special dorsal fin that attracts prey. The fin looks like a fishing lure and is covered in **bioluminescent** bacteria, which glows. Males don't have that feature. They attach to the female to eat.

Harvested to Extinction

Fish are a good source of protein and minerals. But human consumption may be causing their extinction. Scientists estimate that 90 million metric tons of fish are caught each year. This rate is too high to allow fish to repopulate. Fishing in deeper waters reduces rare species and upsets the balance of Earth's food chain. In addition to legal commercial fishing, illegal fishing destroys billions of fish and their habitats.

Some people use aquaculture, or fisheries, to raise fish specifically for food. This helps protect wild fish populations. Below is a map showing the amount of fish, in metric tons, that each region in the world produces through aquaculture.

Aquaculture Production 2002
In Metric Tons, not including plants

- None
- Less than 10,000
- 10,000-150,000
- 150-490,000
- 490-850,000
- 2,200,000 (India)
- 27,800,000 (China)
- No data

Areas of high phytoplankton production

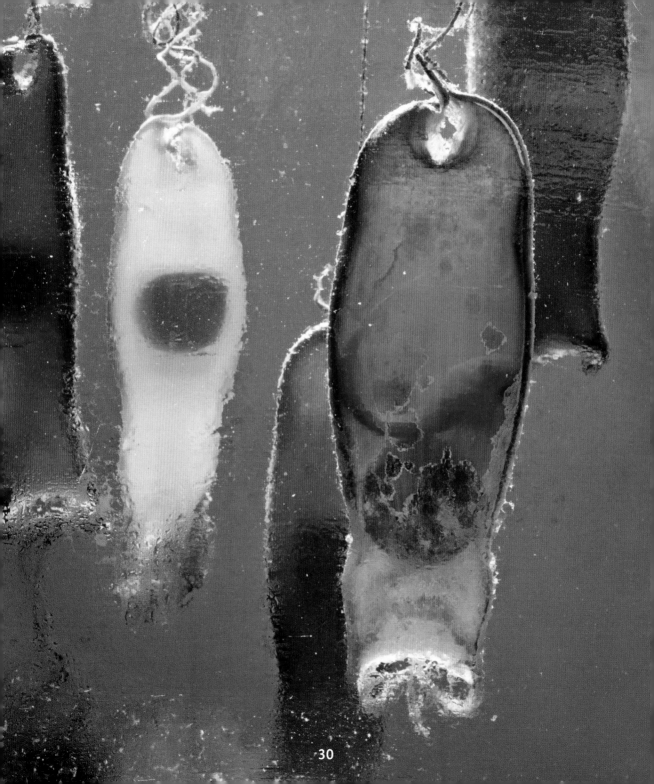

Circle of Life

Some fish are live-bearers, which means the females' eggs are **fertilized** inside her body, and she gives birth to live fish. Other fish are egg layers. The female releases eggs into the water, and the male fertilizes them afterward.

Fish reproduction is known as **spawning**. Some fish, such as lake sturgeon, spawn about every four to six years. Others, such as round goby, spawn multiple times from spring until fall.

The leathery case containing a shark egg is known as a mermaid's purse.

Laying Eggs

Bony fish can lay hundreds to millions of eggs at one time, depending on the species. Because the eggs are vulnerable to predators, including other fish, bony fish sometimes hide the eggs inside crevices, plants, or gravel beds. Young fish mature at different rates. A fish that lives only a year or two will mature and reproduce rapidly. A fish that lives for 80 years may not mature for decades.

It takes about three years for koi to mature.

The oldest known koi lived for 226 years.

From Egg to Fish

A female lays several eggs in a safe place. A male fish fertilizes them.

Larvae hatch from the eggs. These babies are not yet fully developed.

Fully mature fish are able to spawn. They continue to grow slowly throughout their lives.

The young fish develop fins, a skeleton, and scales. The juveniles begin to look more like their parents.

Swimming upstream against a river's current can be difficult.

A Long Way to Travel

Some fish, such as salmon, travel hundreds or thousands of miles to lay eggs in the streams where they were born. After the eggs hatch, the young travel downstream and mature in the ocean waters. A few years later, they swim back upstream to give birth. Pacific salmon die after a single spawning. Atlantic salmon often survive and swim downstream again.

When eels spawn, it is their eggs that make the journey. American and European eels spawn in the Sargasso Sea near Bermuda. The eggs float along the ocean currents while hatching into larvae. The larvae travel for one to three years until they reach the coast. By then, they are juvenile eels called glass eels. The eels migrate to streams and rivers until it is time for them to return to the ocean to lay eggs.

Because they are transparent, juvenile eels are often called glass eels.

Live-Bearers

The eggs of live-bearing fish are fertilized while inside the female's body. Weeks later, the female gives birth to fully formed fish. Some fish, like guppies, do not release all their eggs at the same time. They can store a male's **sperm** and give birth up to three times from one mating.

Most sharks and rays are live-bearers. They give birth to a small number of live young at a time.

Common stingrays usually give birth to between four and seven babies, called pups.

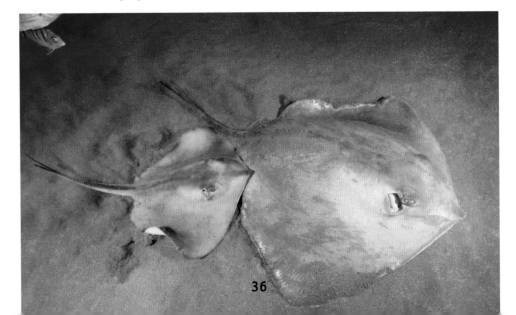

Baby sea horses are usually born after two or three weeks in the father's brood pouch.

A Few Exceptions!

Sea horses are unusual fish. The female deposits her eggs inside the male's pouch. The male fertilizes the eggs and carries them until birth. Because they are poor swimmers, sea horses often mate for life.

Some fish, such as tilapia, are mouth brooders. The male or female collects fertilized eggs after they are deposited and holds them in their mouth until they hatch.

Aquariums can help teach the public about fish conservation.

Endangered Species

The world's population of fish is in danger. More than 85 percent of the species are in decline. Scientists predict that many will be gone in the next 40 years. As species become endangered and face extinction, scientists and government officials study causes and possible solutions. Loss of habitat is one cause of species disappearance. Overfishing and the introduction of **invasive** species are others.

 More than 700 million people visit zoos and aquariums each year.

Problems With People

The greatest threat to fish is from people. Human population growth and an increasing demand for land destroy natural habitats. Toxic runoff from cities and farms pollutes water. This depletes the oxygen in the water and reduces fish populations. Overfishing also affects fish populations. Each year, people consume an average of 37 pounds (16.8 kilograms) of fish. If too many fish are taken out of a habitat, the species may not be able to survive.

Testing the water and surrounding soil allows scientists to keep track of the effects of pollution.

Lionfish are native to the region where the Indian and Pacific Oceans meet.

Humans have introduced invasive species into habitats around the world. Ships pick up invasive species when drawing water for ballast, or stability. These species are released into new environments, where they sometimes multiply quickly, eating native fish and their food supply. The poisonous lionfish is one invasive species. Lionfish are destroying ecosystems from North Carolina to the Caribbean. This invader may have arrived years ago as part of the aquarium trade.

The United States has declared 140,000 square miles (362,598 square kilometers) of ocean near the northwestern Hawaiian Islands a national monument.

Finding Solutions

There is hope. World organizations are springing into action. Scientists count and catalog global fishing stocks. They tag larger species to determine their migration patterns. Scientists also analyze caught fish to track illegal fishing. Governments are limiting commercial fishing and declaring wetlands and other habitats off-limits to development. By 2020, 10 percent of the oceans will be protected as well. Such efforts will lead to a brighter future for fish.

Medical Cures

Zebra fish are not mammals, but they share a lot of traits with them. They have hearts, similar digestive organs, and red blood cells produced in the bones. Scientists at Brigham and Women's Hospital in Boston, Massachusetts, are studying the blood cells of zebra fish. They believe that these studies will lead to medical solutions for people with blood disorders, such as leukemia. ★

Length of smallest fish: Paedocypris progenetica, 0.31 in. (0.79 mm)

Length of largest fish: Whale shark, 40 ft. (12.2 m)

Weight of heaviest fish: Sunfish, 5,071 lb. (2,300 kg)

Longest life span recorded for a fish: Koi, 226 years

Shortest life span recorded for a fish: Pygmy goby, 59 days

Age of oldest known fish fossil found: 530 million years

Length of largest extinct fish: Megalodon shark, 60 ft. (18.3 m)

Did you find the truth?

T Male sea horses give birth instead of females.

F Whales are the largest fish on the planet.

Resources

Books

Johnson, Rebecca L. *Journey into the Deep: Discovering New Ocean Creatures*. Minneapolis: Millbrook, 2011.

Ocean. New York: DK Publishing, 2008.

Patterson, Caroline. *Fish Do What in the Water?* Helena, MT: Farcountry, 2012.

Visit this Scholastic Web site for more information on fish:

★ www.factsfornow.scholastic.com
Enter the keyword **Fish**

Important Words

bioluminescent (by-oh-loo-mih-NESS-uhnt) — describing a living organism able to emit light

camouflage (KAM-uh-flahzh) — a disguise or natural coloring that allows animals to hide by making them look like their surroundings

cartilage (KAHR-tuh-lij) — a strong, elastic tissue that forms the outer ear and nose of humans and other animals, and the skeletons of some fish

fertilized (FUR-tuh-lized) — made able to produce babies

ichthyologists (ik-thee-AH-luh-jists) — scientists who study fish

invasive (in-VAY-siv) — describing a plant or animal that is introduced in to a new habitat and may cause it harm

larvae (LAR-vay) — fish at the stage of development between an egg and a juvenile, before developing skeletons, scales, and fins

spawning (SPAWN-ing) — producing a large number of eggs

sperm (SPURM) — a male reproductive cell that is capable of fertilizing eggs in a female

symbiosis (sim-bee-OH-sus) — a cooperative relationship between two organisms

vertebrates (VUR-tuh-bruts) — animals that have backbones

Index

Page numbers in **bold** indicate illustrations

About the Author

Christine Taylor-Butler is the author of more than 60 books for children, including the True Book series on American History/Government, Health and the Human Body, and Science Experiments. A graduate of the Massachusetts Institute of Technology, Christine holds degrees in both civil engineering and art and design. She currently lives in Kansas City, Missouri.